50 Cozy Pasta Dishes for Comfort Food Lovers

By: Kelly Johnson

Table of Contents

- Pasta with Clams and White Wine Sauce
- Baked Penne with Tomato and Basil
- Pasta with Creamy Pesto and Peas
- Zucchini Noodles with Marinara Sauce
- Pumpkin Pasta with Sage and Parmesan
- Beef Stroganoff with Egg Noodles
- Pasta with Roasted Garlic and Parmesan
- Pasta Salad with Italian Dressing and Veggies
- Creamy Cajun Shrimp Pasta
- Fettuccine with Wild Mushroom Sauce
- Spaghetti with Homemade Meatballs
- Pasta with Creamy Tomato Basil Sauce
- Lobster Pasta with Garlic Butter
- Saffron Risotto with Peas and Parmesan
- Spinach and Ricotta Cannelloni
- Pasta with Anchovy and Breadcrumbs
- Chicken Alfredo Bake with Broccoli
- Baked Spaghetti with Cheese and Meat Sauce
- Farfalle with Asparagus and Lemon Cream Sauce
- Pasta with Roasted Red Pepper Sauce

Creamy Alfredo Fettuccine

Ingredients:

- 12 oz fettuccine pasta
- 1/2 cup butter
- 1 cup heavy cream
- 2 cups grated Parmesan cheese
- 2 garlic cloves, minced
- Salt and pepper to taste
- Chopped parsley for garnish

Instructions:

1. **Cook the Pasta:** Boil fettuccine according to package instructions. Drain and set aside.
2. **Make the Sauce:** In a large skillet, melt butter over medium heat. Add minced garlic and sauté until fragrant. Stir in heavy cream and bring to a simmer.
3. **Combine:** Reduce heat and gradually whisk in Parmesan cheese until melted and smooth. Season with salt and pepper. Add cooked fettuccine and toss to coat.
4. **Serve:** Garnish with chopped parsley before serving.

Classic Bolognese Spaghetti

Ingredients:

- 12 oz spaghetti
- 1 lb ground beef
- 1 onion, chopped
- 2 garlic cloves, minced
- 1 carrot, diced
- 1 celery stalk, diced
- 1 can (14 oz) crushed tomatoes
- 1 tablespoon tomato paste
- 1/2 cup red wine (optional)
- Salt and pepper to taste
- Grated Parmesan cheese for serving

Instructions:

1. **Cook the Pasta:** Prepare spaghetti according to package instructions. Drain and set aside.
2. **Make the Sauce:** In a large skillet, sauté onion, garlic, carrot, and celery until softened. Add ground beef and cook until browned.
3. **Add Tomatoes:** Stir in crushed tomatoes, tomato paste, and red wine. Simmer for 30 minutes. Season with salt and pepper.
4. **Serve:** Toss spaghetti with Bolognese sauce and top with grated Parmesan cheese.

Macaroni and Cheese with Breadcrumb Topping

Ingredients:

- 8 oz elbow macaroni
- 2 cups shredded sharp cheddar cheese
- 1/2 cup milk
- 1/4 cup butter
- 1/4 cup all-purpose flour
- 1/2 teaspoon paprika
- Salt and pepper to taste
- 1 cup breadcrumbs
- 2 tablespoons melted butter (for topping)

Instructions:

1. **Cook the Pasta:** Boil macaroni according to package instructions. Drain and set aside.
2. **Make the Cheese Sauce:** In a saucepan, melt butter. Stir in flour and cook for 1 minute. Gradually whisk in milk and cook until thickened. Stir in cheese, paprika, salt, and pepper.
3. **Combine:** Mix cooked macaroni with cheese sauce and transfer to a baking dish.
4. **Add Topping:** Combine breadcrumbs with melted butter and sprinkle over the macaroni. Bake at 350°F (175°C) for 20 minutes until golden.

Penne Arrabbiata with Spicy Tomato Sauce

Ingredients:

- 12 oz penne pasta
- 3 tablespoons olive oil
- 3 garlic cloves, sliced
- 1/2 teaspoon red pepper flakes
- 1 can (14 oz) crushed tomatoes
- Salt and pepper to taste
- Fresh basil for garnish
- Grated Parmesan cheese for serving

Instructions:

1. **Cook the Pasta:** Boil penne according to package instructions. Drain and set aside.
2. **Make the Sauce:** In a skillet, heat olive oil over medium heat. Sauté sliced garlic and red pepper flakes until fragrant. Add crushed tomatoes and simmer for 15 minutes. Season with salt and pepper.
3. **Combine:** Toss cooked penne with the spicy tomato sauce.
4. **Serve:** Garnish with fresh basil and grated Parmesan cheese.

Lasagna with Ricotta and Spinach

Ingredients:

- 9 lasagna noodles
- 2 cups ricotta cheese
- 2 cups spinach, cooked and chopped
- 2 cups marinara sauce
- 2 cups shredded mozzarella cheese
- 1/2 cup grated Parmesan cheese
- 1 egg
- Salt and pepper to taste

Instructions:

1. **Cook the Noodles:** Prepare lasagna noodles according to package instructions. Drain and set aside.
2. **Prepare the Filling:** In a bowl, mix ricotta cheese, spinach, egg, salt, and pepper.
3. **Assemble the Lasagna:** In a baking dish, spread some marinara sauce, layer 3 noodles, half of the ricotta mixture, and a third of the mozzarella. Repeat layers, finishing with noodles and marinara on top. Sprinkle with remaining mozzarella and Parmesan cheese.
4. **Bake:** Cover with foil and bake at 375°F (190°C) for 30 minutes. Remove foil and bake for an additional 15 minutes until golden.

Mushroom Stroganoff with Egg Noodles

Ingredients:

- 12 oz egg noodles
- 2 tablespoons butter
- 1 onion, chopped
- 2 cups mushrooms, sliced
- 2 garlic cloves, minced
- 1 cup vegetable broth
- 1 cup sour cream
- Salt and pepper to taste
- Chopped parsley for garnish

Instructions:

1. **Cook the Noodles:** Boil egg noodles according to package instructions. Drain and set aside.
2. **Cook the Vegetables:** In a skillet, melt butter. Sauté onion and garlic until softened, then add mushrooms and cook until golden.
3. **Make the Sauce:** Stir in vegetable broth and simmer for 10 minutes. Remove from heat and stir in sour cream. Season with salt and pepper.
4. **Combine:** Toss the sauce with cooked egg noodles and garnish with chopped parsley.

Pasta Carbonara with Pancetta

Ingredients:

- 12 oz spaghetti
- 4 oz pancetta, diced
- 2 eggs
- 1 cup grated Parmesan cheese
- 2 garlic cloves, minced
- Salt and pepper to taste
- Chopped parsley for garnish

Instructions:

1. **Cook the Pasta:** Boil spaghetti according to package instructions. Reserve some pasta water before draining.
2. **Cook the Pancetta:** In a skillet, cook pancetta until crispy. Add minced garlic and cook for an additional minute.
3. **Make the Sauce:** In a bowl, whisk together eggs and Parmesan cheese.
4. **Combine:** Toss hot spaghetti with pancetta and garlic, then quickly stir in the egg mixture, adding reserved pasta water as needed for creaminess. Season with salt and pepper.
5. **Serve:** Garnish with chopped parsley before serving.

Enjoy making and indulging in these delicious pasta dishes!

Pesto Pasta with Cherry Tomatoes

Ingredients:

- 12 oz pasta (e.g., spaghetti or fusilli)
- 1 cup basil pesto
- 2 cups cherry tomatoes, halved
- 1/4 cup grated Parmesan cheese
- Salt and pepper to taste
- Fresh basil for garnish

Instructions:

1. **Cook the Pasta:** Boil pasta according to package instructions. Drain and reserve some pasta water.
2. **Combine:** In a large bowl, mix cooked pasta with pesto and cherry tomatoes. If the mixture is too thick, add reserved pasta water a little at a time.
3. **Season:** Add salt and pepper to taste.
4. **Serve:** Top with grated Parmesan cheese and garnish with fresh basil before serving.

Baked Ziti with Sausage and Mozzarella

Ingredients:

- 12 oz ziti pasta
- 1 lb Italian sausage, casings removed
- 2 cups marinara sauce
- 2 cups shredded mozzarella cheese
- 1 cup ricotta cheese
- 1/2 cup grated Parmesan cheese
- 1 teaspoon Italian seasoning
- Salt and pepper to taste

Instructions:

1. **Cook the Pasta:** Boil ziti according to package instructions until al dente. Drain and set aside.
2. **Cook the Sausage:** In a skillet, cook sausage until browned. Stir in marinara sauce and Italian seasoning.
3. **Assemble:** In a baking dish, mix cooked ziti with sausage sauce, ricotta cheese, and half of the mozzarella.
4. **Top and Bake:** Sprinkle remaining mozzarella and Parmesan on top. Bake at 375°F (190°C) for 25-30 minutes until bubbly and golden.

Creamy Garlic Butter Pasta

Ingredients:

- 12 oz pasta (e.g., fettuccine or spaghetti)
- 1/2 cup butter
- 4 garlic cloves, minced
- 1 cup heavy cream
- 1 cup grated Parmesan cheese
- Salt and pepper to taste
- Chopped parsley for garnish

Instructions:

1. **Cook the Pasta:** Boil pasta according to package instructions. Drain and set aside.
2. **Make the Sauce:** In a large skillet, melt butter over medium heat. Add minced garlic and sauté until fragrant. Stir in heavy cream and bring to a simmer.
3. **Combine:** Gradually whisk in Parmesan cheese until melted and smooth. Season with salt and pepper. Toss in cooked pasta until well coated.
4. **Serve:** Garnish with chopped parsley before serving.

Fusilli with Roasted Butternut Squash and Sage

Ingredients:

- 12 oz fusilli pasta
- 2 cups butternut squash, cubed
- 2 tablespoons olive oil
- 1 tablespoon fresh sage, chopped (or 1 teaspoon dried sage)
- 1/2 cup grated Parmesan cheese
- Salt and pepper to taste

Instructions:

1. **Roast the Squash:** Preheat the oven to 400°F (200°C). Toss butternut squash with olive oil, sage, salt, and pepper. Spread on a baking sheet and roast for 20-25 minutes until tender.
2. **Cook the Pasta:** Boil fusilli according to package instructions. Drain and set aside.
3. **Combine:** In a large bowl, mix roasted squash with cooked pasta. Add grated Parmesan and toss to combine.
4. **Serve:** Garnish with additional sage and Parmesan cheese before serving.

Shrimp Scampi with Linguine

Ingredients:

- 12 oz linguine
- 1 lb shrimp, peeled and deveined
- 4 tablespoons butter
- 4 garlic cloves, minced
- 1/2 cup white wine (optional)
- Juice of 1 lemon
- 1/4 cup chopped parsley
- Salt and pepper to taste

Instructions:

1. **Cook the Pasta:** Boil linguine according to package instructions. Drain and set aside.
2. **Cook the Shrimp:** In a large skillet, melt butter over medium heat. Add garlic and sauté until fragrant. Add shrimp and cook until pink.
3. **Make the Sauce:** Stir in white wine and lemon juice, simmering for 2-3 minutes. Season with salt and pepper.
4. **Combine:** Toss cooked linguine with shrimp and sauce. Garnish with chopped parsley before serving.

Vegetable Primavera with Olive Oil

Ingredients:

- 12 oz pasta (e.g., penne or fettuccine)
- 2 tablespoons olive oil
- 1 zucchini, sliced
- 1 bell pepper, sliced
- 1 cup cherry tomatoes, halved
- 1 cup broccoli florets
- 2 garlic cloves, minced
- Salt and pepper to taste
- Grated Parmesan cheese for serving

Instructions:

1. **Cook the Pasta:** Boil pasta according to package instructions. Drain and set aside.
2. **Sauté the Vegetables:** In a large skillet, heat olive oil over medium heat. Add garlic and sauté until fragrant. Add zucchini, bell pepper, broccoli, and cherry tomatoes. Cook until vegetables are tender.
3. **Combine:** Toss cooked pasta with sautéed vegetables. Season with salt and pepper.
4. **Serve:** Top with grated Parmesan cheese before serving.

One-Pot Cheesy Taco Pasta

Ingredients:

- 12 oz pasta (e.g., rotini or penne)
- 1 lb ground beef or turkey
- 1 packet taco seasoning
- 3 cups chicken broth
- 1 can (15 oz) diced tomatoes
- 1 cup shredded cheddar cheese
- 1 cup corn (fresh, canned, or frozen)
- Chopped cilantro for garnish

Instructions:

1. **Cook the Meat:** In a large pot, brown ground beef or turkey over medium heat. Drain excess fat.
2. **Add Ingredients:** Stir in taco seasoning, chicken broth, diced tomatoes, and pasta. Bring to a boil, then reduce heat and simmer until pasta is cooked, about 10-12 minutes.
3. **Add Cheese and Corn:** Stir in shredded cheese and corn until melted and combined.
4. **Serve:** Garnish with chopped cilantro before serving.

Enjoy making and indulging in these delicious pasta dishes!

Pasta e Fagioli (Pasta and Beans)

Ingredients:

- 1 cup ditalini pasta
- 1 can (15 oz) cannellini beans, drained and rinsed
- 1 can (14 oz) diced tomatoes
- 1 onion, chopped
- 2 carrots, chopped
- 2 celery stalks, chopped
- 4 cups vegetable broth
- 2 garlic cloves, minced
- 1 teaspoon dried oregano
- Salt and pepper to taste
- Fresh parsley for garnish

Instructions:

1. **Sauté Vegetables:** In a large pot, heat olive oil over medium heat. Add onion, carrots, and celery, and sauté until softened.
2. **Add Garlic and Seasoning:** Stir in garlic, oregano, salt, and pepper, cooking for 1-2 minutes until fragrant.
3. **Simmer:** Add diced tomatoes and vegetable broth, bringing the mixture to a boil. Reduce heat and simmer for 15 minutes.
4. **Cook Pasta and Beans:** Add ditalini pasta and cannellini beans. Cook until pasta is al dente, about 8-10 minutes.
5. **Serve:** Garnish with fresh parsley before serving.

Pasta Puttanesca with Olives and Capers

Ingredients:

- 12 oz spaghetti
- 2 tablespoons olive oil
- 4 garlic cloves, minced
- 1 can (14 oz) diced tomatoes
- 1/2 cup black olives, pitted and sliced
- 2 tablespoons capers, rinsed
- 1 teaspoon red pepper flakes
- Fresh parsley for garnish
- Salt and pepper to taste

Instructions:

1. **Cook the Pasta:** Boil spaghetti according to package instructions. Drain and set aside.
2. **Sauté Garlic:** In a large skillet, heat olive oil over medium heat. Add garlic and red pepper flakes, sautéing until fragrant.
3. **Add Sauce Ingredients:** Stir in diced tomatoes, olives, and capers. Simmer for 10 minutes, allowing flavors to meld.
4. **Combine:** Toss cooked spaghetti with the sauce, ensuring pasta is well coated. Season with salt and pepper.
5. **Serve:** Garnish with fresh parsley before serving.

Spaghetti Aglio e Olio with Chili Flakes

Ingredients:

- 12 oz spaghetti
- 1/2 cup olive oil
- 6 garlic cloves, thinly sliced
- 1 teaspoon red pepper flakes (adjust to taste)
- Salt to taste
- Fresh parsley, chopped for garnish
- Grated Parmesan cheese (optional)

Instructions:

1. **Cook the Pasta:** Boil spaghetti according to package instructions. Reserve 1/2 cup of pasta water, then drain.
2. **Sauté Garlic:** In a large skillet, heat olive oil over medium heat. Add sliced garlic and red pepper flakes, cooking until garlic is golden (be careful not to burn).
3. **Combine:** Add drained spaghetti to the skillet, tossing to coat. If needed, add reserved pasta water to create a silky sauce.
4. **Serve:** Season with salt and garnish with chopped parsley and grated Parmesan cheese, if desired.

Baked Mac and Cheese with Gruyère

Ingredients:

- 8 oz elbow macaroni
- 2 tablespoons butter
- 2 tablespoons all-purpose flour
- 2 cups milk
- 2 cups shredded Gruyère cheese
- 1 cup shredded cheddar cheese
- 1/2 teaspoon mustard powder
- Salt and pepper to taste
- 1 cup breadcrumbs

Instructions:

1. **Cook the Pasta:** Boil elbow macaroni according to package instructions. Drain and set aside.
2. **Make Cheese Sauce:** In a saucepan, melt butter over medium heat. Stir in flour and cook for 1 minute. Gradually whisk in milk, cooking until thickened. Stir in Gruyère, cheddar, mustard powder, salt, and pepper until melted.
3. **Combine:** In a large bowl, mix cooked pasta with cheese sauce.
4. **Bake:** Transfer to a greased baking dish, top with breadcrumbs, and bake at 350°F (175°C) for 25-30 minutes until golden and bubbly.

Pasta alla Norma with Eggplant

Ingredients:

- 12 oz penne or rigatoni
- 1 eggplant, diced
- 2 cups marinara sauce
- 2 tablespoons olive oil
- 2 garlic cloves, minced
- 1/2 teaspoon dried oregano
- Salt and pepper to taste
- 1/2 cup ricotta cheese
- Fresh basil for garnish

Instructions:

1. **Prepare Eggplant:** Sprinkle diced eggplant with salt and let sit for 30 minutes to draw out moisture. Rinse and pat dry.
2. **Cook the Pasta:** Boil pasta according to package instructions. Drain and set aside.
3. **Sauté Eggplant:** In a skillet, heat olive oil over medium heat. Add eggplant and cook until golden and tender. Add garlic, oregano, salt, and pepper, cooking for another 1-2 minutes.
4. **Combine:** Stir in marinara sauce and cooked pasta, tossing to combine.
5. **Serve:** Top with dollops of ricotta cheese and garnish with fresh basil before serving.

Lemon Ricotta Pasta with Fresh Herbs

Ingredients:

- 12 oz pasta (e.g., fettuccine or linguine)
- 1 cup ricotta cheese
- Zest and juice of 1 lemon
- 1/2 cup grated Parmesan cheese
- 1/4 cup fresh basil, chopped
- 1/4 cup fresh parsley, chopped
- Salt and pepper to taste

Instructions:

1. **Cook the Pasta:** Boil pasta according to package instructions. Reserve some pasta water, then drain.
2. **Make the Sauce:** In a large bowl, combine ricotta, lemon zest, lemon juice, and Parmesan cheese. Add reserved pasta water to achieve desired creaminess.
3. **Combine:** Toss cooked pasta with the ricotta mixture, adding fresh herbs, salt, and pepper.
4. **Serve:** Garnish with additional herbs and Parmesan cheese before serving.

Creamy Spinach and Artichoke Pasta

Ingredients:

- 12 oz pasta (e.g., penne or farfalle)
- 1 cup frozen spinach, thawed and drained
- 1 can (14 oz) artichoke hearts, drained and chopped
- 2 tablespoons olive oil
- 2 garlic cloves, minced
- 1 cup cream cheese
- 1/2 cup grated Parmesan cheese
- Salt and pepper to taste

Instructions:

1. **Cook the Pasta:** Boil pasta according to package instructions. Drain and set aside.
2. **Sauté Vegetables:** In a large skillet, heat olive oil over medium heat. Add garlic and sauté until fragrant. Stir in spinach and artichokes, cooking for 2-3 minutes.
3. **Make the Sauce:** Add cream cheese and Parmesan, stirring until melted and creamy. Season with salt and pepper.
4. **Combine:** Toss cooked pasta with the creamy mixture until well coated.
5. **Serve:** Garnish with additional Parmesan cheese before serving.

Enjoy cooking and savoring these delicious pasta dishes!

Fettuccine with Lemon Garlic Shrimp

Ingredients:

- 12 oz fettuccine
- 1 lb shrimp, peeled and deveined
- 3 tablespoons olive oil
- 4 garlic cloves, minced
- Zest and juice of 1 lemon
- 1/4 teaspoon red pepper flakes
- Salt and pepper to taste
- Fresh parsley for garnish

Instructions:

1. **Cook the Fettuccine:** Boil fettuccine according to package instructions. Drain and set aside, reserving 1/2 cup of pasta water.
2. **Sauté Shrimp:** In a large skillet, heat olive oil over medium heat. Add minced garlic and red pepper flakes, cooking until fragrant (about 1 minute).
3. **Add Shrimp:** Add shrimp to the skillet, seasoning with salt and pepper. Cook until shrimp are pink and opaque, about 3-4 minutes.
4. **Combine:** Stir in the cooked fettuccine, lemon zest, lemon juice, and reserved pasta water. Toss to combine and heat through.
5. **Serve:** Garnish with fresh parsley before serving.

Pasta with Sausage and Broccoli Rabe

Ingredients:

- 12 oz pasta (e.g., orecchiette or penne)
- 1 lb Italian sausage, casings removed
- 1 bunch broccoli rabe, trimmed and chopped
- 3 garlic cloves, minced
- 1/2 teaspoon red pepper flakes
- 1/4 cup olive oil
- Salt and pepper to taste
- Grated Parmesan cheese for serving

Instructions:

1. **Cook the Pasta:** Boil pasta according to package instructions. Drain and set aside.
2. **Cook Sausage:** In a large skillet, heat olive oil over medium heat. Add sausage, breaking it up with a spoon, and cook until browned.
3. **Add Garlic and Broccoli Rabe:** Stir in garlic and red pepper flakes, cooking for 1-2 minutes. Add broccoli rabe, cooking until tender (about 5 minutes).
4. **Combine:** Add cooked pasta to the skillet, tossing to combine. Season with salt and pepper.
5. **Serve:** Top with grated Parmesan cheese before serving.

Cheesy Spinach and Mushroom Pasta Bake

Ingredients:

- 12 oz pasta (e.g., rotini or penne)
- 2 cups fresh spinach, chopped
- 8 oz mushrooms, sliced
- 2 cups marinara sauce
- 1 cup ricotta cheese
- 1 cup shredded mozzarella cheese
- 1/2 cup grated Parmesan cheese
- 2 tablespoons olive oil
- Salt and pepper to taste

Instructions:

1. **Cook the Pasta:** Boil pasta according to package instructions. Drain and set aside.
2. **Sauté Vegetables:** In a skillet, heat olive oil over medium heat. Add mushrooms and cook until browned. Stir in spinach, cooking until wilted.
3. **Combine:** In a large bowl, mix cooked pasta, sautéed vegetables, marinara sauce, ricotta, salt, and pepper.
4. **Bake:** Transfer to a greased baking dish, top with mozzarella and Parmesan cheese, and bake at 350°F (175°C) for 25-30 minutes until bubbly and golden.
5. **Serve:** Let cool slightly before serving.

Balsamic Glazed Pasta with Roasted Vegetables

Ingredients:

- 12 oz pasta (e.g., farfalle or penne)
- 2 cups mixed vegetables (e.g., bell peppers, zucchini, cherry tomatoes)
- 3 tablespoons olive oil
- 1/4 cup balsamic vinegar
- 1 tablespoon honey
- Salt and pepper to taste
- Fresh basil for garnish

Instructions:

1. **Roast Vegetables:** Preheat oven to 425°F (220°C). Toss mixed vegetables with 2 tablespoons olive oil, salt, and pepper. Spread on a baking sheet and roast for 20-25 minutes until tender.
2. **Cook the Pasta:** Boil pasta according to package instructions. Drain and set aside.
3. **Make Balsamic Glaze:** In a small saucepan, combine balsamic vinegar and honey. Simmer over medium heat until thickened.
4. **Combine:** In a large bowl, toss cooked pasta with roasted vegetables and balsamic glaze.
5. **Serve:** Garnish with fresh basil before serving.

Tortellini Soup with Spinach and Tomatoes

Ingredients:

- 12 oz cheese tortellini
- 4 cups vegetable or chicken broth
- 1 can (14 oz) diced tomatoes
- 2 cups fresh spinach
- 2 garlic cloves, minced
- 1 teaspoon dried oregano
- Salt and pepper to taste
- Grated Parmesan cheese for serving

Instructions:

1. **Cook the Tortellini:** Boil tortellini according to package instructions. Drain and set aside.
2. **Make the Soup:** In a large pot, combine broth, diced tomatoes, garlic, oregano, salt, and pepper. Bring to a simmer.
3. **Add Spinach and Tortellini:** Stir in fresh spinach and cooked tortellini. Simmer for another 5 minutes until heated through.
4. **Serve:** Garnish with grated Parmesan cheese before serving.

Pasta with Sun-Dried Tomatoes and Goat Cheese

Ingredients:

- 12 oz pasta (e.g., linguine or spaghetti)
- 1/2 cup sun-dried tomatoes, chopped
- 4 oz goat cheese
- 2 tablespoons olive oil
- 2 garlic cloves, minced
- 1/2 teaspoon dried basil
- Salt and pepper to taste
- Fresh basil for garnish

Instructions:

1. **Cook the Pasta:** Boil pasta according to package instructions. Drain and set aside.
2. **Sauté Garlic and Tomatoes:** In a skillet, heat olive oil over medium heat. Add garlic and sun-dried tomatoes, cooking for 2-3 minutes.
3. **Combine:** Add cooked pasta to the skillet, tossing with goat cheese, dried basil, salt, and pepper.
4. **Serve:** Garnish with fresh basil before serving.

Egg Noodles with Chicken and Gravy

Ingredients:

- 12 oz egg noodles
- 2 cups cooked chicken, shredded
- 2 cups chicken broth
- 1/2 cup milk
- 1/4 cup flour
- 1/4 cup butter
- Salt and pepper to taste

Instructions:

1. **Cook the Egg Noodles:** Boil egg noodles according to package instructions. Drain and set aside.
2. **Make Gravy:** In a saucepan, melt butter over medium heat. Whisk in flour, cooking for 1-2 minutes. Gradually add chicken broth and milk, whisking until thickened.
3. **Combine:** Stir in shredded chicken and cooked egg noodles. Season with salt and pepper.
4. **Serve:** Serve warm, garnished with parsley if desired.

Enjoy these delicious pasta dishes!

Cajun Chicken Pasta with Cream Sauce

Ingredients:

- 12 oz penne pasta
- 1 lb chicken breast, sliced
- 2 tablespoons Cajun seasoning
- 3 tablespoons olive oil
- 1 cup heavy cream
- 1/2 cup chicken broth
- 1 cup bell peppers, sliced
- 1/2 cup onion, sliced
- 2 garlic cloves, minced
- Salt and pepper to taste
- Fresh parsley for garnish

Instructions:

1. **Cook the Pasta:** Boil penne pasta according to package instructions. Drain and set aside.
2. **Season the Chicken:** In a bowl, toss chicken slices with Cajun seasoning.
3. **Sauté Chicken:** In a large skillet, heat olive oil over medium heat. Add seasoned chicken and cook until browned and cooked through (about 5-7 minutes). Remove from skillet and set aside.
4. **Sauté Vegetables:** In the same skillet, add bell peppers, onion, and garlic. Sauté until softened.
5. **Make the Sauce:** Pour in heavy cream and chicken broth, bringing to a simmer. Return chicken to the skillet and combine.
6. **Combine:** Toss in cooked pasta, mixing until well coated. Season with salt and pepper.
7. **Serve:** Garnish with fresh parsley before serving.

Stuffed Shells with Marinara Sauce

Ingredients:

- 12 oz jumbo pasta shells
- 2 cups ricotta cheese
- 1 cup shredded mozzarella cheese
- 1/2 cup grated Parmesan cheese
- 1 egg, beaten
- 2 cups marinara sauce
- 1 teaspoon dried basil
- Salt and pepper to taste

Instructions:

1. **Cook the Shells:** Boil pasta shells according to package instructions. Drain and set aside.
2. **Prepare Filling:** In a bowl, mix ricotta, 1/2 cup mozzarella, Parmesan, egg, basil, salt, and pepper until well combined.
3. **Stuff Shells:** Preheat oven to 375°F (190°C). Fill each shell with the ricotta mixture and place in a greased baking dish.
4. **Add Marinara Sauce:** Pour marinara sauce over stuffed shells and sprinkle with remaining mozzarella cheese.
5. **Bake:** Cover with foil and bake for 25 minutes. Remove foil and bake for an additional 10 minutes until cheese is bubbly and golden.
6. **Serve:** Let cool slightly before serving.

Pasta with Clams and White Wine Sauce

Ingredients:

- 12 oz spaghetti
- 2 cans (6.5 oz each) chopped clams, drained (reserve liquid)
- 1 cup white wine
- 4 garlic cloves, minced
- 1/4 cup olive oil
- 1/4 teaspoon red pepper flakes
- 1/4 cup fresh parsley, chopped
- Salt and pepper to taste
- Lemon wedges for serving

Instructions:

1. **Cook the Pasta:** Boil spaghetti according to package instructions. Drain and set aside.
2. **Sauté Garlic:** In a large skillet, heat olive oil over medium heat. Add garlic and red pepper flakes, cooking until fragrant (about 1 minute).
3. **Add Wine and Clams:** Pour in white wine and bring to a simmer. Add chopped clams and reserved liquid, cooking for an additional 5 minutes.
4. **Combine:** Add cooked spaghetti to the skillet, tossing to combine. Season with salt, pepper, and fresh parsley.
5. **Serve:** Serve with lemon wedges for squeezing over the pasta.

Baked Penne with Tomato and Basil

Ingredients:

- 12 oz penne pasta
- 2 cups marinara sauce
- 1 cup ricotta cheese
- 1 cup shredded mozzarella cheese
- 1/2 cup grated Parmesan cheese
- 1/4 cup fresh basil, chopped
- Salt and pepper to taste

Instructions:

1. **Cook the Pasta:** Boil penne pasta according to package instructions. Drain and set aside.
2. **Combine Ingredients:** In a large bowl, mix cooked pasta, marinara sauce, ricotta cheese, half of the mozzarella, basil, salt, and pepper.
3. **Transfer to Baking Dish:** Preheat oven to 350°F (175°C). Pour the mixture into a greased baking dish. Top with remaining mozzarella and Parmesan cheese.
4. **Bake:** Bake for 25-30 minutes until the cheese is melted and bubbly.
5. **Serve:** Let cool for a few minutes before serving.

Pasta with Creamy Pesto and Peas

Ingredients:

- 12 oz pasta (e.g., rotini or fettuccine)
- 1 cup heavy cream
- 1/2 cup pesto sauce
- 1 cup frozen peas, thawed
- Salt and pepper to taste
- Grated Parmesan cheese for serving

Instructions:

1. **Cook the Pasta:** Boil pasta according to package instructions. Drain and set aside.
2. **Make the Sauce:** In a skillet, combine heavy cream and pesto, heating over low until warmed through.
3. **Combine:** Add cooked pasta and peas to the sauce, tossing to coat. Season with salt and pepper.
4. **Serve:** Serve topped with grated Parmesan cheese.

Zucchini Noodles with Marinara Sauce

Ingredients:

- 4 medium zucchinis, spiralized
- 2 cups marinara sauce
- 2 tablespoons olive oil
- 2 garlic cloves, minced
- Salt and pepper to taste
- Fresh basil for garnish

Instructions:

1. **Sauté Zucchini Noodles:** In a skillet, heat olive oil over medium heat. Add garlic and sauté for 1 minute. Add spiralized zucchini and cook for 3-5 minutes until just tender.
2. **Add Marinara Sauce:** Pour marinara sauce over zucchini noodles, cooking until heated through. Season with salt and pepper.
3. **Serve:** Garnish with fresh basil before serving.

Pumpkin Pasta with Sage and Parmesan

Ingredients:

- 12 oz pasta (e.g., fettuccine or penne)
- 1 cup pumpkin puree
- 1/2 cup heavy cream
- 1/4 cup grated Parmesan cheese
- 1 tablespoon fresh sage, chopped (or 1 teaspoon dried sage)
- Salt and pepper to taste
- Toasted pumpkin seeds for garnish

Instructions:

1. **Cook the Pasta:** Boil pasta according to package instructions. Drain and set aside.
2. **Make the Sauce:** In a skillet, combine pumpkin puree, heavy cream, sage, salt, and pepper. Heat over low until warmed through.
3. **Combine:** Add cooked pasta to the sauce, tossing to coat. Stir in Parmesan cheese.
4. **Serve:** Garnish with toasted pumpkin seeds before serving.

Enjoy these delicious pasta dishes!

Beef Stroganoff with Egg Noodles

Ingredients:

- 12 oz egg noodles
- 1 lb beef sirloin, sliced into thin strips
- 1 medium onion, diced
- 2 garlic cloves, minced
- 8 oz mushrooms, sliced
- 1 cup beef broth
- 1 cup sour cream
- 2 tablespoons Worcestershire sauce
- 2 tablespoons olive oil
- Salt and pepper to taste
- Fresh parsley for garnish

Instructions:

1. **Cook the Noodles:** Boil egg noodles according to package instructions. Drain and set aside.
2. **Sauté Beef:** In a large skillet, heat olive oil over medium-high heat. Add beef strips, cooking until browned (about 3-4 minutes). Remove and set aside.
3. **Sauté Vegetables:** In the same skillet, add onions and garlic, cooking until softened. Add mushrooms and cook until they release their moisture.
4. **Make the Sauce:** Stir in beef broth, Worcestershire sauce, salt, and pepper. Bring to a simmer and reduce slightly.
5. **Finish the Dish:** Lower the heat and stir in sour cream. Return the beef to the skillet and combine with the sauce.
6. **Combine:** Toss the cooked egg noodles with the beef mixture.
7. **Serve:** Garnish with fresh parsley before serving.

Pasta with Roasted Garlic and Parmesan

Ingredients:

- 12 oz pasta (e.g., spaghetti or linguine)
- 1 head garlic
- 1/4 cup olive oil
- 1/2 cup grated Parmesan cheese
- Salt and pepper to taste
- Fresh parsley for garnish

Instructions:

1. **Roast the Garlic:** Preheat oven to 400°F (200°C). Slice the top off the garlic head and drizzle with olive oil. Wrap in foil and roast for 30-35 minutes until soft.
2. **Cook the Pasta:** Boil pasta according to package instructions. Reserve 1/2 cup pasta water and drain.
3. **Make the Sauce:** Squeeze the roasted garlic into a bowl and mash. Mix in olive oil, Parmesan, and reserved pasta water until combined.
4. **Combine:** Toss the pasta with the garlic mixture, adding salt and pepper to taste.
5. **Serve:** Garnish with fresh parsley before serving.

Pasta Salad with Italian Dressing and Veggies

Ingredients:

- 12 oz pasta (e.g., rotini or penne)
- 1 cup cherry tomatoes, halved
- 1 cup cucumber, diced
- 1/2 cup bell peppers, diced
- 1/4 cup red onion, thinly sliced
- 1/2 cup black olives, sliced
- 1/2 cup Italian dressing
- Salt and pepper to taste
- Fresh basil for garnish

Instructions:

1. **Cook the Pasta:** Boil pasta according to package instructions. Drain and let cool.
2. **Combine Ingredients:** In a large bowl, mix cooked pasta with cherry tomatoes, cucumber, bell peppers, red onion, and olives.
3. **Add Dressing:** Pour Italian dressing over the pasta salad, tossing to combine. Season with salt and pepper.
4. **Serve:** Garnish with fresh basil before serving.

Creamy Cajun Shrimp Pasta

Ingredients:

- 12 oz pasta (e.g., fettuccine)
- 1 lb shrimp, peeled and deveined
- 1 tablespoon Cajun seasoning
- 2 tablespoons olive oil
- 1 cup heavy cream
- 1/2 cup grated Parmesan cheese
- 2 cloves garlic, minced
- 1/2 cup green onions, chopped
- Salt and pepper to taste

Instructions:

1. **Cook the Pasta:** Boil pasta according to package instructions. Drain and set aside.
2. **Season the Shrimp:** Toss shrimp with Cajun seasoning.
3. **Sauté Shrimp:** In a large skillet, heat olive oil over medium heat. Add shrimp and cook until pink and opaque (about 3-4 minutes). Remove and set aside.
4. **Make the Sauce:** In the same skillet, add garlic and sauté until fragrant. Stir in heavy cream and Parmesan cheese, simmering until slightly thickened.
5. **Combine:** Add cooked pasta and shrimp to the sauce, mixing well. Season with salt and pepper.
6. **Serve:** Garnish with green onions before serving.

Fettuccine with Wild Mushroom Sauce

Ingredients:

- 12 oz fettuccine
- 8 oz mixed wild mushrooms, sliced
- 1 cup heavy cream
- 1/2 cup grated Parmesan cheese
- 1/4 cup white wine
- 2 tablespoons olive oil
- 2 garlic cloves, minced
- Salt and pepper to taste
- Fresh parsley for garnish

Instructions:

1. **Cook the Fettuccine:** Boil fettuccine according to package instructions. Drain and set aside.
2. **Sauté Mushrooms:** In a large skillet, heat olive oil over medium heat. Add mushrooms and cook until browned (about 5-7 minutes).
3. **Add Garlic and Wine:** Stir in garlic and white wine, cooking until wine is reduced.
4. **Make the Sauce:** Pour in heavy cream, simmering until thickened. Stir in Parmesan cheese, seasoning with salt and pepper.
5. **Combine:** Toss the cooked fettuccine with the mushroom sauce.
6. **Serve:** Garnish with fresh parsley before serving.

Spaghetti with Homemade Meatballs

Ingredients:

- 12 oz spaghetti
- 1 lb ground beef
- 1/2 cup breadcrumbs
- 1/4 cup grated Parmesan cheese
- 1 egg
- 2 cloves garlic, minced
- 2 cups marinara sauce
- Salt and pepper to taste
- Fresh basil for garnish

Instructions:

1. **Cook the Spaghetti:** Boil spaghetti according to package instructions. Drain and set aside.
2. **Make the Meatballs:** In a bowl, mix ground beef, breadcrumbs, Parmesan, egg, garlic, salt, and pepper. Form into meatballs.
3. **Cook the Meatballs:** In a skillet, brown meatballs on all sides. Add marinara sauce, simmering until meatballs are cooked through.
4. **Combine:** Toss cooked spaghetti with marinara sauce and meatballs.
5. **Serve:** Garnish with fresh basil before serving.

Pasta with Creamy Tomato Basil Sauce

Ingredients:

- 12 oz pasta (e.g., penne)
- 1 can (14 oz) crushed tomatoes
- 1 cup heavy cream
- 1/2 cup grated Parmesan cheese
- 2 cloves garlic, minced
- 1 teaspoon dried basil
- Salt and pepper to taste
- Fresh basil for garnish

Instructions:

1. **Cook the Pasta:** Boil pasta according to package instructions. Drain and set aside.
2. **Make the Sauce:** In a skillet, sauté garlic in olive oil until fragrant. Add crushed tomatoes, heavy cream, dried basil, salt, and pepper. Simmer until thickened.
3. **Combine:** Stir in cooked pasta and Parmesan cheese, mixing well.
4. **Serve:** Garnish with fresh basil before serving.

Enjoy these delicious pasta recipes!

Lobster Pasta with Garlic Butter

Ingredients:

- 8 oz pasta (e.g., linguine or fettuccine)
- 1 lb lobster meat, cooked and chopped
- 4 tablespoons unsalted butter
- 4 cloves garlic, minced
- 1/2 teaspoon red pepper flakes (optional)
- 1/2 cup heavy cream
- 1/2 cup grated Parmesan cheese
- Salt and pepper to taste
- Fresh parsley for garnish

Instructions:

1. **Cook the Pasta:** Boil pasta according to package instructions. Drain and reserve a little pasta water.
2. **Make Garlic Butter:** In a large skillet, melt butter over medium heat. Add minced garlic and red pepper flakes, cooking until fragrant (about 1-2 minutes).
3. **Add Lobster:** Stir in the chopped lobster meat, cooking until heated through.
4. **Make the Sauce:** Add heavy cream and bring to a simmer. Stir in Parmesan cheese until melted and smooth.
5. **Combine:** Toss the cooked pasta with the lobster and sauce, adding reserved pasta water as needed to thin the sauce.
6. **Serve:** Season with salt and pepper, and garnish with fresh parsley before serving.

Saffron Risotto with Peas and Parmesan

Ingredients:

- 1 cup Arborio rice
- 4 cups chicken or vegetable broth
- 1/2 cup white wine
- 1 small onion, finely chopped
- 2 cloves garlic, minced
- 1/2 cup frozen peas
- 1/2 teaspoon saffron threads
- 1/2 cup grated Parmesan cheese
- 2 tablespoons olive oil
- Salt and pepper to taste
- Fresh parsley for garnish

Instructions:

1. **Prepare Broth:** In a saucepan, heat broth and keep it warm on low heat.
2. **Sauté Vegetables:** In a large skillet, heat olive oil over medium heat. Add onion and garlic, cooking until softened.
3. **Toast Rice:** Add Arborio rice to the skillet, stirring for 2-3 minutes until lightly toasted.
4. **Add Wine and Saffron:** Pour in white wine and saffron, stirring until absorbed.
5. **Add Broth:** Gradually add warm broth, one ladle at a time, stirring frequently until the liquid is absorbed before adding more. Continue until the rice is creamy and cooked (about 18-20 minutes).
6. **Finish the Risotto:** Stir in frozen peas and Parmesan cheese, mixing until melted. Season with salt and pepper.
7. **Serve:** Garnish with fresh parsley before serving.

Spinach and Ricotta Cannelloni

Ingredients:

- 12 cannelloni tubes
- 2 cups ricotta cheese
- 2 cups fresh spinach, chopped
- 1/2 cup grated Parmesan cheese
- 1 egg
- 2 cups marinara sauce
- 1 teaspoon dried Italian herbs
- Salt and pepper to taste
- Fresh basil for garnish

Instructions:

1. **Preheat Oven:** Preheat the oven to 375°F (190°C).
2. **Prepare Filling:** In a bowl, mix ricotta, spinach, Parmesan, egg, dried herbs, salt, and pepper until well combined.
3. **Stuff Cannelloni:** Fill each cannelloni tube with the ricotta mixture.
4. **Prepare Baking Dish:** Spread 1 cup of marinara sauce in the bottom of a baking dish. Place stuffed cannelloni on top and cover with remaining sauce.
5. **Bake:** Cover with foil and bake for 25-30 minutes. Remove foil and bake for an additional 10 minutes until bubbly.
6. **Serve:** Garnish with fresh basil before serving.

Pasta with Anchovy and Breadcrumbs

Ingredients:

- 12 oz pasta (e.g., spaghetti or linguine)
- 4 anchovy fillets, chopped
- 2 tablespoons olive oil
- 2 cloves garlic, minced
- 1/2 cup breadcrumbs
- 1/4 teaspoon red pepper flakes (optional)
- 1/2 cup parsley, chopped
- Salt and pepper to taste
- Lemon wedges for serving

Instructions:

1. **Cook the Pasta:** Boil pasta according to package instructions. Reserve some pasta water and drain.
2. **Sauté Anchovies:** In a large skillet, heat olive oil over medium heat. Add anchovies and cook until they dissolve, about 2 minutes.
3. **Add Garlic:** Stir in garlic and red pepper flakes, cooking for an additional minute.
4. **Add Breadcrumbs:** Mix in breadcrumbs, toasting until golden brown.
5. **Combine:** Add cooked pasta to the skillet along with reserved pasta water, tossing to combine. Stir in parsley and season with salt and pepper.
6. **Serve:** Serve with lemon wedges.

Chicken Alfredo Bake with Broccoli

Ingredients:

- 12 oz penne pasta
- 2 cups cooked chicken, shredded
- 2 cups broccoli florets
- 2 cups Alfredo sauce
- 1 cup shredded mozzarella cheese
- 1/2 cup grated Parmesan cheese
- 1 teaspoon garlic powder
- Salt and pepper to taste

Instructions:

1. **Preheat Oven:** Preheat the oven to 375°F (190°C).
2. **Cook the Pasta:** Boil penne according to package instructions. Add broccoli during the last 3 minutes of cooking. Drain and set aside.
3. **Mix Ingredients:** In a large bowl, combine cooked pasta, broccoli, shredded chicken, Alfredo sauce, garlic powder, salt, and pepper.
4. **Transfer to Baking Dish:** Pour mixture into a greased baking dish and top with mozzarella and Parmesan cheese.
5. **Bake:** Bake for 25-30 minutes until bubbly and golden on top.
6. **Serve:** Let cool slightly before serving.

Baked Spaghetti with Cheese and Meat Sauce

Ingredients:

- 12 oz spaghetti
- 1 lb ground beef
- 2 cups marinara sauce
- 1/2 cup grated Parmesan cheese
- 2 cups shredded mozzarella cheese
- 1 small onion, diced
- 2 cloves garlic, minced
- 1 teaspoon Italian seasoning
- Salt and pepper to taste

Instructions:

1. **Preheat Oven:** Preheat the oven to 350°F (175°C).
2. **Cook the Spaghetti:** Boil spaghetti according to package instructions. Drain and set aside.
3. **Make Meat Sauce:** In a skillet, cook ground beef, onion, and garlic over medium heat until meat is browned. Drain excess fat, then add marinara sauce, Italian seasoning, salt, and pepper. Simmer for 5 minutes.
4. **Combine Ingredients:** In a large bowl, mix cooked spaghetti with meat sauce and half of the mozzarella cheese.
5. **Transfer to Baking Dish:** Pour mixture into a greased baking dish and top with remaining mozzarella and Parmesan cheese.
6. **Bake:** Bake for 20-25 minutes until cheese is bubbly and golden.
7. **Serve:** Let cool slightly before serving.

Farfalle with Asparagus and Lemon Cream Sauce

Ingredients:

- 12 oz farfalle pasta
- 1 lb asparagus, trimmed and cut into pieces
- 1 cup heavy cream
- 1/2 cup grated Parmesan cheese
- 2 tablespoons lemon juice
- 2 tablespoons olive oil
- 2 cloves garlic, minced
- Salt and pepper to taste
- Lemon zest for garnish

Instructions:

1. **Cook the Pasta:** Boil farfalle according to package instructions. Add asparagus during the last 2-3 minutes of cooking. Drain and set aside.
2. **Make the Sauce:** In a large skillet, heat olive oil over medium heat. Add garlic and sauté until fragrant. Pour in heavy cream, stirring to combine.
3. **Add Cheese and Lemon:** Stir in Parmesan cheese and lemon juice, cooking until cheese melts and sauce thickens slightly.
4. **Combine:** Toss the cooked pasta and asparagus in the sauce, seasoning with salt and pepper.
5. **Serve:** Garnish with lemon zest before serving.

Pasta with Roasted Red Pepper Sauce

Ingredients:

- 12 oz pasta (e.g., penne or fettuccine)
- 2 cups roasted red peppers, jarred or homemade
- 1/2 cup heavy cream
- 1/2 cup grated Parmesan cheese
- 2 cloves garlic, minced
- 2 tablespoons olive oil
- Salt and pepper to taste
- Fresh basil for garnish

Instructions:

1. **Cook the Pasta:** Boil pasta according to package instructions. Drain and set aside.
2. **Make the Sauce:** In a blender, combine roasted red peppers, heavy cream, garlic, salt, and pepper. Blend until smooth.
3. **Heat the Sauce:** In a skillet, heat olive oil over medium heat. Pour in the blended sauce and simmer for 5-7 minutes.
4. **Add Cheese:** Stir in Parmesan cheese until melted and combined.
5. **Combine:** Toss cooked pasta in the sauce until evenly coated.
6. **Serve:** Garnish with fresh basil before serving.

Enjoy your delightful pasta dishes!